UNDERSTANDING

THE

POWER

OF

Choice

PUBLICATION

Typeset in cambria by Letsu Samuel Yayra of Sky-Mc Ventures, Legon, Accra.

Tel.: 050 464 1608

Edited by D.N.A. Addy, DANDY Books, Oyibi, Accra.

Tel.:024 320 4375

Printed and bound by the University of Ghana Printing Press, Legon, Accra Ghana.

Tel.: 030 293 4987

TABLE OF CONTENTS

DEDICATION

This book is dedicated to
JERRY MENSAH ADUKPO

ACKNOWLEDGEMENT

I wish to acknowledge the good and wonderful works of God in my life. The protection and great ideas for the preparation of this book could not have come from anybody but Him. Hallelujah!

The instrumental support of the Ghana Armed Forces, especially the Air Force, through the following personalities: AVM Frank Hanson (Chief of Air Staff), the Directors – AFHQ, the Base Commander (Air Commodore Joshua Lartei Mensah-Larkai), WG CDR Antwi (Officer Commanding the Flying Wing – Air Force Base, Accra), SWO Gasu Bright (of blessed memory), WOI Awittor Doris (OPS I/C, Air Force Headquaters), WOI Afriyie Patrick (OPS I/C, Air Force Base, Accra), WO I Kyere Kofi Brantuo. To All and Sundry, who contributed in one way or the other to the success of this book, by way of advice, mentorship, guidance and support.

My Grandparents, Mr. Mensah Adukpo and Madam Ruth Akuwor Mego, who have played instrumental roles in my early childhood development. Their efforts made me who I am today.

My parents, Mr. Gabriel Adukpo and Madam Agnes Ashiabi, for their relentless efforts in seeing me through school, even in the face of insufficiency. I really appreciate their efforts.

To the rest of my family – Victoria, Samuel, Cephas, James, Ebenezer, Akpene, Sampson, Ken, Kelvin, Bill – to mention but a few, my fondest regards.

To Gertrude Amuzu, for her encouragement and support throughout my times of trouble and frustrations.

To my Intake Ghana Air Force Recruit CSE 1/2013, and the 2007/2008 Batch of Wesley Grammar School, Blessed Generation International School 2005 Batch and the Tsawoenu D/A JHS 2005 Batch.

LAC Yin Thomas Sungure and Emmanuel Megbenu, for their immense support and contribution to the success of this book.

TO ALL THOSE WHOSE NAMES I HAVE NOT MENTIONED, I have not forgotten your contribution and pieces of advice through it all.

Your sacrificial efforts and investments in my work and life will never be forgotten. God richly bless you all.

FOREWORD

Some many years ago, during the "Common Entrance" days, before you gained admission into the Secondary school, we were given a card that contained the list of all the secondary schools in Ghana that could aid the potential student to choose the specific second cycle institution one desired. We were asked to take it home for a specific period for parental guidance.

With the euphoria of going to secondary school, I gladly gave the card to my father to help me select the kind of school he wanted me to attend since he was my sole sponsor. To my amazement, my father told me to make the choice myself since I was going to write the exam and knew my capabilities and that he was going to support the choice I made.

Growing up, I had seen most of my seniors transform shortly after returning on mid-terms from school with some haircuts such as 7Up, ponk, half bowl among others, and also a drastic change in appearance and demeanor. I was enthused about those traits and decided to follow the status quo.

I chose Koforidua Secondary Technical school because my friend's father schooled there and was a pilot in the Ghana Airforce. That initial opportunity to make a choice of my own ushered me into the position of responsibility. I made the choice of KSTS and that has remained the catalyst to my life changing advancement till date and I have never regretted it although there were very challenging times. I carried along the sense of responsibility knowing very well that i had no excuse to give for failure. I had the freedom to inner peace of mind and to learn with the freedom to embrace the future. Today I am a proud product of the University of Ghana and an accomplished airman of the Ghana air force. The choice I made had the power to make me who I am today than if I had listened to my step mum who had other advices for me.

This book is unique for several whys and wherefores. The author of this book has characterized his write up with varied real-life decision making and a guide that has the power to make very positive impacts and transform the reader to different and dynamic levels of attainment. He has also given us an insight as to the parameters we need to set in order to achieve revolutionary goals with careful analytic kind of the choice we make. To those of us who have difficulty in making brave choices, this is a complete, prolific and brilliant write up by Mensah Adukpo Prince that serves a guide and guard going in to the future. To the guardian, it aids you in handling and dealing with the choices made by the youngsters. A must-read masterpiece.

Afriyie Patrick (WO I)
BA (HONS) PSYCHOLOGY
In Charge of Operations,
President of WO'S and SNCO'S MESS
Airforce Base Accra.

PREFACE

Do you know the number one reason why many people are not able to achieve their aim in life, nor reach their target as well as life goals?

It is their inability to make the right choices at the right time when the opportunity is available. Those who do not make the right choices struggle. They struggle through life without a sense of fulfillment.

On the other hand, people who make the right choices, based on certain principles, prosper and can achieve their life goals. They feel fulfilled and accomplished at the slightest opportunity. One of the greatest powers of great men is the ability to make the right choices and at the right times.

Whatever you want, the power of choice will help you achieve it. In the power of choice, you will realise, among other things, the need to focus on your strengths, recognise the weaknesses in your decision and choice making. It is good to know that common sense and ethical values can co-exist.

In this book you will realise simple and amazing revelations, ideas and principles that will benefit everyone who implements them in the choice making process. These strategies will enrich your ability to make the right choices.

Your choice will determine your future – learn how to make it now.

To live is to choose. But to choose well, you must know where you are and what you stand for, where you want to go and why you want to go there.

BUSUMURU KOFI ANNAN

-   7TH UN SEC GENERAL

PROLOGUE

CHOICES

The laws of dialectics define the unity of opposites in the whole and also show that choices are inevitable in the course of life.

However, choices by themselves do not determine the outcome of human enterprises and are not made consciously all the time.

What really determine outcomes is the extent to which excellence is pursued and the level of restraining factors needing to be overcome in the pursuit of human goals.

I am unable to say with any level of certainty that, I am the product of the choices I have made in life. This is because I do not think making deliberate and conscious choices has been part of my life story.

The point is that even if I made deliberate and conscious choices in my life, I would hesitate to claim that I am a successful example to be emulated by others.

While many of my peers went through education and became holders of PHDs, I only ended up with a diploma from the Ghana Institute of Journalism. I cannot be counted amongst the wealthiest of my peers. I am not the healthiest of my peers and I am certainly not the most accomplished in any sphere of life.

I am the Editor of "The Insight", established in 1993, simply because the Newspaper Licensing Decree had been repealed at the time and friends and well-wishers provided the means to build that institution.

Today, I am a director and majority shareholder in Pan African Television, not because I made ay conscious choice but because, the people around me; family, relatives and comrades provided tremendous assistance and urged me on.

Some gave out the brain and muscle power for free, others contributed financial resources and from some of them, I simply stole their ideas about the role of the media in the creation of a more just and equitable world.

Yes, I agree that life is itself a choice and it involves picking and choosing. Indeed, we are alive today because we chose not to commit suicide but life is not just about choices.

I am deeply impressed by the attempt of the author to place choice at the centre of happenings in life but it will not tell my story.

Comr'd. Kwesi Pratt
Editor of "THE INSIGHT" and
DIRECTOR, PAN AFRICAN TELEVISION NETWORK.

'THE POWER OF CHOICE'

'I can tell you that, what you are and have now is because of the choices and decisions you made years ago. Your status quo today is because of the choices you made yesterday. You are the true picture of the choices you made'.

The
Power
Of
Choice
OPTION A
OPTION B
OPTION C
OPTION D
OPTION E

CHAPTER 1

WHAT IS A CHOICE

It is everyone's dream to succeed in life. However only few people understand the underlining principles of success. It is good to know certain principles to guide you in your journey through life. These principles do not only lead an individual to success, but also help an individual to attain the fulfillment and satisfaction required for pure joy and total peace.

The basic and most important cause of a successful and fulfilled life is the choice an individual makes. Research has shown that making good choices play a pivotal role in an individual's journey through life.

One can make a choice between imagined options, which is what to do if a situation or an unforeseen circumstance is met. One can also make choices based on real actions and expected outcomes. For instance, a traveler might choose a route for a journey based on the preference of arriving at a given destination as soon as possible. Another traveler may also choose a different route, based on the preference for safety and recreation. In all these, remember that choices are made, but based on different cognition, instinct, need and feeling.

'Choice making' may be defined as the act of picking or deciding between two or more possibilities. It may also be considered as the opportunity or power of selection.

Choice involves decision-making. It can include judging the merits of multiple options and selecting one or more of them. You need to understand that you are the major determinant of whatever you become. Once your choice is made your success is majorly guaranteed, if you stay focused and follow through with a well thought-out action plan. Your future is based on your decisions hence you need to choose wisely. Remember that once you make the choice of what you want, the path to achieving it becomes clearer. You have very great potentials but once you have not made any choice, they remain either a theory or fantasy. Know that the day you make the choice of what you want, you have taken the very first step to achieving it. Also remember that, it is your choice that controls your life and thought patterns. Until the right choice is made, everything else remains barren and impossible to achieve. Choices are so important that, until you begin to choose, your destiny will remain blurred. This is because, your choices inform your habit and your habit determines your destiny. Take it without doubt that no one can put you down if you choose to remain standing and no man can shatter your dreams if you make the choice to keep your dreams alive.

Successful people have become what they are because of the choices they made, while others either made the wrong choices or have not made any choice at all. Failure does not just happen to anyone. It results from conscious and unconscious neglect of making the right choices. Men and women who have made it in life have repeatedly made choices which have favoured them. They did not just sit in and wait for success to catch up with them, or for their luck to shine. Once you make the choice for success your progress becomes unstoppable.

CHAPTER 2

LIFE IS ABOUT CHOICES, RECOGNISE YOURSELF AND CHOOSE RIGHT

Every choice an individual makes is aimed at a desired, good, and fulfilled life. Please understand that the results you are currently experiencing in your life are absolutely perfected for you by your earlier choices. This includes your career, personal relationships, and financial status.

How could it be otherwise? The reason you are where you are in life, is simply as a result of the choices you made to this point. When you accept total responsibility of this fact, you are well on your way to enjoying total peace of mind. Many people endure a life filled with frustration because they are stuck in satisfying the choices or requirements of other people who are happily enjoying their own lives because of their own choices.

You will hear people say mostly in frustration, "Let me do this and that to please him/her, let me do his will so that he can love me, let me impress him/her, let me try to please him/her, let me make him/her happy".

These are the various reasons many people give for abandoning their own carefully selected choices which are based on their strengths and weaknesses. They tend to make decisions based on the expectation of other people. If you are in such a situation, it is time you respect your own choice and work to accomplish what you wish for. Your choices are as equally good as the ones being suggested. Make your own choice and own the copyright; it's the best for you. Take note that, I don't seek to infer, by any means, that one should not take good advice, rather don't let any form of advice derail you from working towards your own positive agenda.

When you say things like "she made me angry", believe me, she did not, you chose to be angry instead of making a different choice of allowing sleeping dogs lie.

You will hear other popular comments like, "I'm stuck in the relationship" Who told you that? Is the relationship a ditch that you will get stuck in? "I hate this job"! Believe me, it's your choice to quit it and nobody can do that for you. "I'm having difficulty with this course"; or "that course is too difficult"! Who told you that? Do you know that other people are finding it easy and are happy doing that same course you claim is too difficult? The reason is simple, it is not because they are smarter or more intelligent than you. They are happy with it and finding it more understanding, because they made the choice to do that course, based on their assessment of their own strengths and weaknesses. Everyone is unique in their own

special way. You are unique. Make your own choice and you will be surprised at the outcome. You don't have to enroll for further studies in high schools and Universities because your colleagues at work are doing same. You know yourself and you know that you do better in business than at studies. So why waste your business capital on school fees and fail the course? Why don't you start your own business and when the graduates are looking for job, you will employ them as a business owner. It is all a matter of knowing oneself and making the right choices. When someone is forcing a choice on you, always remember that you are different, and you have different weaknesses and strengths.

When Robert Nesta Marley, in his *Redemption Song* he said, "Emancipate yourself from mental slavery" he simply emphasized that as an individual, you should free yourself from unnecessarily pleasing people, no matter what they mean or which role they play in your life. Make a choice to do what you want to do and do it with pride, dignity, and all seriousness.

You will succeed! You will be free and happy in life!

I hope that by this information, you will be able to understand yourself, make good choices and stay focused and that will propel you to your own desired status and echelon in life.

CHAPTER 3

THE ART OF CHOICE MAKING

Making choices and decisions are a part of life. Simply put, the way life unfolds, with its twists and turns, starts and stops, requires us to make choices and decisions every step of the way. It is therefore disturbing and saddening that, by the time young people have reached adulthood, many have not mastered the art of decision-making. In fact, many people dread change because this means they will have to contemplate something different from what they are used to and may even be required to make a change. Why is this so?

Well, there may be many reasons and factors that determine why some people can just dive into life and do what is required with enthusiasm and excitement, while others are paralyzed at the thought of having to step up to anything that might require taking action. A person's temperament, their disposition or nature may contribute to the way they view life. Some people are fearless, enjoying risk and adventure, while others fear undertaking change and making mistakes, preferring to stay close to what is familiar and not wandering too far---and that includes their choices and decisions.

Some people have been burned in the past by poor choices and decisions and are afraid to, once again, risk making a bad choice or decision. They may do nothing hoping the change will work itself out, or go away, or that somebody else will take care of what needs to be done.

Then there's the issue of children never learning to make decisions because they have never been taught how to do it; many of the important choices have been made for them and they may simply have no say in the matter. That may be the fault of parents who try to control too much of their children's lives, fearing that they will miss out on what they, the parents, deem to be important unless they jump in to ensure the "proper" course for their children. The bottom line is that decision-making is something we all need to learn to do. This very essential life skill should be taught from a very early age since decision-making takes years of practice

to master. Learning how to make good choices and wise decisions depends upon several factors: a person's developmental stage/age, having a general idea of right and wrong, and that is in the broadest moral sense since individuals may acquire their own idea of what is right and wrong as they mature and understand what the decision-making process entails.

You may think starting with infants is just too early but that's not the case. It's good practice to reinforce behavior that is unacceptable or potentially harmful. For example, when a baby begins to crawl, finds small objects or dirt on the floor and mouths it, it is appropriate not only to remove the object but to say, "No" and tell the baby why putting this object in their mouth isn't okay. Even though a baby may not initially understand what you're saying, by hearing it repeatedly they will start to make the connection and understand that all behaviours have consequences some good, some bad.

Toddlers need to be given controlled options. For example, offer the child a choice between two things only. "Do you want cereal or eggs; milk or juice?" "Do you want to wear the green shirt with these blue pants or this dress with leggings?" This allows the youngster to have a voice in making choices that fit into your choices and routine.

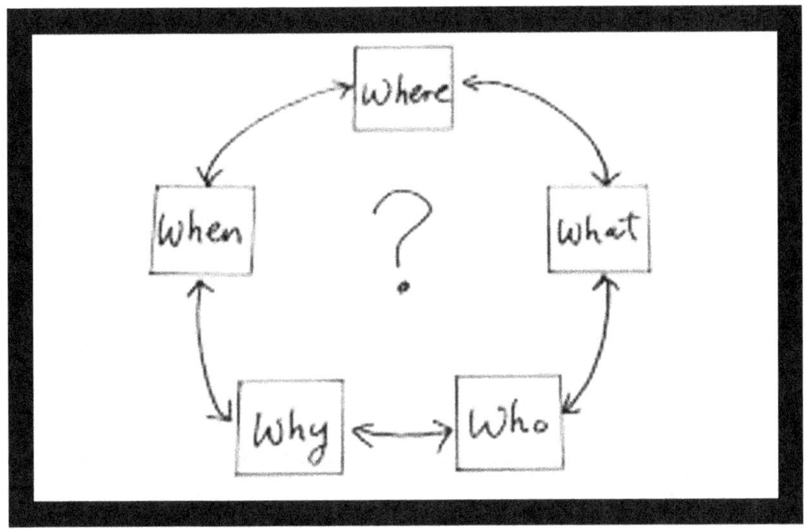

CHAPTER 4

CHOICE AND SELF-DISCIPLINE

Staying in one's boundary is one of the major challenges when it comes to the issue of choice. It is worth noting that staying within one's own choice is a matter of discipline. That means being more conscious of the everyday activities that you choose to spend your time on. To avoid drifting away from your choices, you need to constantly remind yourselves of your choices and why you are taking actions to achieve them. It also means saying no to a lot more options that will be available. Many people are drifted away from the choices they have made upon several considerations just because someone has convinced them to do so. Remember that if you remain focused on your choice, knowing your needs and strengths, you will not be swayed.

One major challenge of choice making is not the inability but the temptation of being swayed away from ones choice due to several factors, including pressure from people, economic situations and social exigencies.

Being swayed from your choice can have dire consequences on an individual, including total loss of focus and sense of direction. Please, do well to live within your choice and this requires a lot more than the decision. It is said that, climbing to the top is not as difficult as maintaining your status up there. It is the same way when it comes to choices. One can easily make a choice but staying within the choice made is where the difficulty lies. To be able to stay within one's own boundary of choice, there's the need to acquire the skills of making life's choices and before, that is self-discipline.

You need to know your passion. Do not let the fear of your dad push you to abandon your passion. If your passion is not Science, then join the Arts. If it is not Arts join the Business class and if it is not Business, then marry Home Economics. Just do well to follow your talent and passion and be comfortable.

Permit me to ask this question, what if Michael Jackson's dad had forced him to become a boxer and Mohammed Ali's dad forced him to become a musician; what if Michael Essien or Asamoah Gyan's parents forced them to become movie stars; and what if Shatta Wale and Stonebouy's parents forced them to become politicians?

You can imagine the disaster in their lives. One simple belief is the answer to all these: make your passion your profession.

CHAPTER 5

RECOGNISING SIMPLE AND COMPLEX CHOICES

Choices may either be simple or complex. Simple choices may include what to eat for dinner or what to wear on a Sunday morning. Simple choices have relatively low impact on the choice maker's life.

More complex choices might involve more than just preference and personal likes or dislikes. For example, complex choices might include what candidate to vote for in an election, what profession to pursue, a life partner, among others. These choices are not based on individual or personal sentiments, but on multiple influences that have larger ramification.

Most people regard having choices as a good thing, although a severely limited or artificially restricted choice can lead to discomfort with choosing and possibly an unsatisfactory outcome. In contrast, a choice with excessively numerous options may lead to confusion, regret of the alternatives not taken and indifference in an amorphous survival.

Just as there is order of life, choice making is no exception. One must develop from one stage to another. That means the individual must master the art of making simple choices, before progressing to more difficult and complex choices. Due to the importance of choices, it's important that parents begin to teach their wards how to make choices from infancy so that by the time they attain adulthood they might have mastered the art.

Some actions when taken by parents will end up equipping their ward with the skill of making choices in the future without difficulty, and to be able to live independently as a confident decision maker without being misled or confused by peers.

Sometimes, people make the wrong choices at the right time. Others also make the right choices at the wrong time. However, there is no difference between these two choices. Sometimes these choices are either made from ignorance or for immediate gratification.

The following are principles that an individual must consider in making choices:

1. You need to appreciate the importance of choice making. Remind yourself that you need to make the right choice at the right time. Always keep it at the back of your mind that, a choice made may make or unmake your whole life.

2. Know your purpose and make the decision to achieve that purpose. Accept what you want to do in life and appreciate it. Broaden your knowledge about that purpose and open yourself to information about your choice.

3. Think thoroughly about your purpose, considering your strengths and weaknesses and assessing your capabilities and incapability. Recognise yourself and appreciate your own self, and that will make you to either make or unmake a decision of choice.

4. Good choices made at the wrong time become wrong choices. It is very important to note that, the first step to the discovery of one's purpose is to first of all make the choice. What your purpose is and how to advance your steps to achieving it is a matter of choice.

Remember that the art of choice making is as old as humanity. That's why it's so important that it must be mastered by everyone who wants to feel fulfilled in life. This is because it borders on all aspects of economic, religion, relationship, career, among others.

Children are not exempted from the choice making process. They should be guided to make simple choices. Parents or guardians can help in building the choice making capabilities of their wards through the following ways:

1. Offer choices/options that are reasonable and readily available to young children.

   Tasks should not be out of their range developmentally. For example, create small jobs that allow your youngster to work beside you, such as dusting the furniture, adding an ingredient or two to a recipe, choosing food at the supermarket, etc. When the child moves into the stage of "I can do it myself," let them try, with your **observation** and **supervision.**

2. Foster responsibility by allowing the child to do some chores/jobs on their own; for example, picking up their toys, feeding the family pet, etc.

3. Break down tasks into smaller pieces or steps, showing children that there is an order to how things are accomplished.

4. Encourage, especially when a child is frustrated or loses patience.

5. Offer praise; get excited for a job well-done, especially when it is the accomplishment of a brand-new skill,

such as dressing themselves, riding a bike, or staying dry through the night.

6. For pre-schoolers, expand the number of choices. As a child gets older, their capacity to understand the difference between right and wrong increases as well as their ability to understand the consequences of their behaviour.

7. Frame choices using key words that are simple to understand, such as: "Do you think this is a good idea/decision/choice, or maybe not the best?": Do you have a better idea, or want to make a different decision/choice?

8. Ask questions to help the child understand various possibilities: "What do you think will happen if you decide to do---?" "How will you feel if you do---?" If doing something involves someone else, such as a friend or a sibling, you can ask the child, "How do you think they will feel as a result of---?

9. Include your child's ideas or opinions when it comes to making family decisions. The child will feel heard, their opinion will be appreciated, and their confidence to express themselves will be nurtured. They will also begin to understand that there is a process involved in decision-making.

10. For school-age children expand the horizon of choices you give them. Expand the importance of the decisions they choose to make. This includes their activities, their friends, school curriculum, educational obligation and personal choices, such as when to go to sleep, style of

clothing to buy, pursuit of personal interests such as music, movies, books, and pursuit of special talents and creative abilities, such as sports and art.

Of course, you as the adult may still make a lot of the important decisions regarding children, but it's essential to give them the chance to learn for themselves.

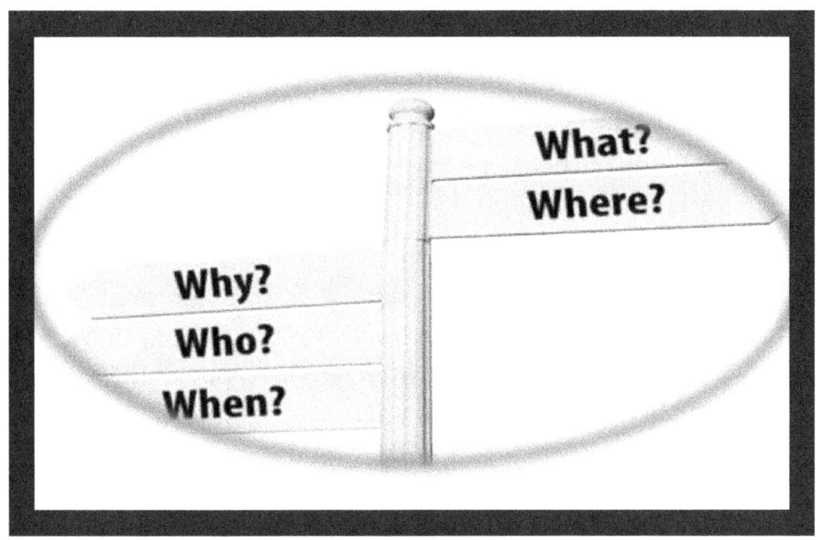

CHAPTER 6

STAGES INVOLVED IN MAKING A GOOD CHOICE

The following are very important stages to consider in making a good choice. Every good choice by any individual may have gone through at least one or more of the following stages:

- Define the issue. Include the need/reason for the decision.

- Brainstorm for possible options and solutions.

- Discuss the options, and their potential consequences, and then narrow down to not more than three choices.

- Pick one of the three choices, formulate an action plan, and follow through.

- Evaluate the solution. If the solution is satisfactory, your child will have a sense of accomplishment. If not satisfactory, or it falls short of expectation, or is just a bad idea, reconsider other choices/possibilities that may bring a better outcome.

- Be available to your child. Talk about issues or problems arising from a decision and encourage them. Lend support, especially in light of a poor decision. Making some bad decisions is part of the maturation process.

- Teens and young adults should be encouraged. Encourage them to expand their choices and decisions. Recognise that adolescents want to have more control over their lives. They want more independence, more time with friends, and more fun. Encourage your young adult to independently practice decision-making skills whenever possible, with you watching on the sideline. When you single handedly continue to make choices and decisions important to your child, you undermine his/her self-esteem and confidence.

- Remember that no one is expected to get things right all the time. We often don't ... but, having some idea of what to do will help to make the big choices and decisions easier. Good decision-making is one of the most important life skills to own and one of the greatest legacies to bequeath a child.

Do you want to succeed? Then this is the principle. You can write this down and use it as a guideline to achieve your aim and succeed in life.

1. Make better choices everyday

Ask yourself this question severally when you are faced with issues of choice! *Do I really want this choice, and do I have the capacity to achieve it?*

2. Develop better habits

Habits are also a matter of choices. Good or bad habits, whether they will help in you achieving your aim, is also a matter of choice.

Choose the right habits and you will succeed.

3. Build a better character

You need to recognise your positive and negative characters and work on them. Do away with the negative characters and concentrate on the positive ones. That will take you very far in life.

Remember that life is a series of Choices. Always choose wisely.

CHAPTER 7

CHOICES AND RESULTS

Many people make choices for immediate gratification forgetting that those choices will have consequences on their future and that of others. Negative choices breed negative consequences. Your choices will determine your quality of life. If you want to have good health and enjoy longevity, you need to make the right choices of which food to eat and what not to eat.

I can tell you that, what you are and have now is because of the choices and decisions you made years ago. Who you are today is a result of the choices you made yesterday. You are the picture of the choices you made. Never doubt the fact that your choices can make or break you. The most important thing in life is recognising the right choices and making those choices at the right time. Remember "recognising your own choices" and not "what some individual or others think is the best or right for you". That is not to say that you should not take advice from people or take the opinions of others about which choices to make in your life. Know and understand yourself better so that you may not be manipulated into making those choices that may result in retrogression and stagnation, instead of progress and advancement. Recognise your strengths and weaknesses and make choices that will project your strengths over your weaknesses, and not vice versa.

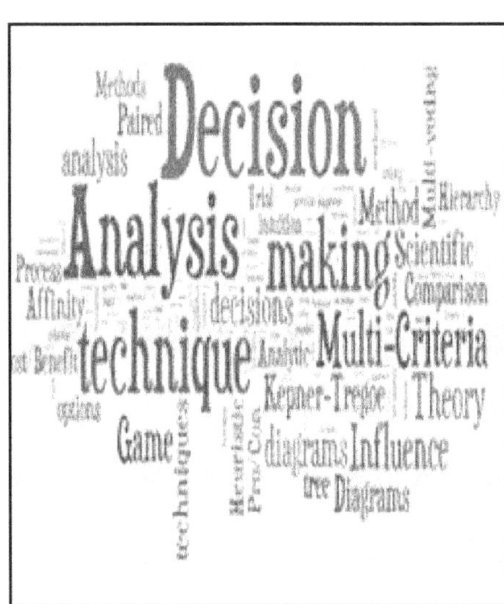

Life is made up of an infinite amount of choices. Most decisions, such as what you'll eat for lunch today, are small and only slightly impactful, but it's the big decisions, the ones that can change your life forever, that are tough to make. But let me hasten to say that, the big decisions depend largely on those slightly impactful ones, which in a way may be considered unimportant. This has only emphasized the critical fact that a momentary decision or choice can affect one's life, hence the need to master the art in order not to make too many errors. If you choose to confront the options before you with courage and confidence, you open yourself to a fulfilling path of your own design, filled with numerous possibilities. Rather than procrastinate in fear of making the wrong decision, weigh your options and act on the best one. Revel in the chance to create the life you want to live. Stop over thinking it. To inspire your next big decision, this is what the great men have to say:

- "Sometimes it's the smallest decisions that can change your life forever."
  — Keri Russell

- "We are the creative force of our life, and through our own decisions rather than our conditions, if we carefully learn to do certain things, we can accomplish those goals."
  — Stephen Covey

- "Your life changes the moment you make a new, congruent, and committed decision."
  — Tony Robbins

- "Life presents you with so many decisions. A lot of times, they're right in front of your face and they're really difficult, but we must make them."
  —Brittany Murphy

- "Choices are the hinges of destiny."
  — Edwin Markham

- "I believe that we are solely responsible for our choices, and we have to accept the consequences of every deed, word, and thought throughout our lifetime."
  —Elisabeth Kubler-Ross

- "I think that there is something beautiful about mortality. It makes our decisions mean more."
  — Brandon Boyd

- "It doesn't matter which side of the fence you get off sometimes. What matters most is getting off. You cannot make progress without making decisions."
  — Jim Rohn

- "Life is a matter of choices, and every choice you make makes you."
  — John C. Maxwell

- "The more decisions that you are forced to make alone, the more you are aware of your freedom to choose."
  — Thornton Wilder

- "The key to accepting responsibility for your life is to accept the fact that your choices, every one of them, are leading you inexorably to either success or failure, however you define those terms."
  — Neal Boortz.

These quotes from these great men can help to inspire you to make a choice and work towards it. The quotes above look at stories and experiences of many people from different areas of life, about the short- and long-term impact of choices on their life. These piece of advice from them will guide young people in making decisions and to remind you of some simple but powerful choices to make in order to take control of your life and make the best out of it.

CHAPTER 8

CHOICE, PARENTING AND GUARDIANSHIP

People who are of much influence in the lives of others must also take this advice into much consideration. Do not force an individual into making a choice against his wish, not even your son or daughter or student. They may end up blaming you or making negative references to such decisions you made for them no matter how successful they may become. There is a great difference between success and fulfillment. One may be successful but unfulfilled, but one cannot be fulfilled and not feel successful. Allow them to play the leading role in making the choices of their lives. You may suggest to them and throw light on the potentials and opportunities in certain areas, but not to force them into accepting and going by your choice. Those are your choices based on your personal interests and strengths. Let them also make their choices taking into consideration their own strengths, weaknesses and interests.

All aspects of life dwell on choices. The decision of whom to marry (love), number of children, education, career, business, religion and even friends are all a matter of choices which, if made wrongly or made at the wrong time, can have dire consequences on the individual in the long run. To have a successful life means making the appropriate choices at the right time.

It is so hard when you think about how to achieve your dreams but very easy when you make the appropriate choices at the right time. This is what is important; life does not just happen to you. It's all about choices and how you respond to every situation. If you are in the habit of continually making the wrong choices, disaster often occurs.

Your everyday choices ultimately determine whether you end up living with abundance or living in poverty. However, life never completely closes the door to opportunities. That is to say that, when you recognise your wrong choices and make the right amends, you can completely change your story and new opportunities will never cease to present themselves unto you. The right and consistent choices lay the foundation for your habits and your habits play a major role in how your future unfolds.

CHAPTER 9

WORDS FROM OUR MENTORS

Jamie Thompson writes on the accounts of some successful people. How their personal choices and decisions changed their story and how such personal introspective choices contributed to their success stories. These are the true accounts of entrepreneurs, authors, musicians, TV personalities and inspirational leaders. A life is made, of a million decisions. There are forks in the road that require a choice: Do I want to be a lawyer or a film producer? Should I travel across the world to attend College? Do I need to stop drinking? Should I take the lucrative job offer if it means spending less time with my family? Sometimes, we know the answers intuitively and quickly decide. Other times, we debate endlessly, agonising our way toward an answer. At pivotal points in life, the number of decisions can be overwhelming. Robert Frost suggested that the best path is the less predictable one. 'Two roads diverged in a wood, and I took the one less traveled by, and that has made all the difference'. That was true for some of the achievers I've read about. Taking risks lead to fantastic success. But, according to others also, well-worn paths work too. That's why choosing can be so difficult; but here are what some choice-makers described as their best choices, how they were made, and how those choices helped lead them toward success and happiness.

BLAKE SHELTON

Country music star and The Voice judge. The best decision I ever made was two weeks out of high school I moved to Nashville to pursue my dream of being a country singer. I think if I hadn't made that decision at such a young age, I might have been afraid to do it later on in life.

JAMES PATTERSON

Best-selling author who released his book entitled 'Filthy Rich'. I'd like to think I've occasionally made good decisions in my life (first among them marrying my wife, Sue)— but professionally, I'd say that leaving my post as North American CEO of J. Walter Thompson. At the time I left, I was being considered as a candidate for worldwide CEO, and it's scary to contemplate a second career when you're doing that well. But I knew I never truly had a passion for advertising. As a business, I'd always found it more difficult than it had to be—it's surprisingly hard to sell clients blueprints that communicate what a television campaign is going to look like before it's filmed. And every client you deal with is very different than the last. Leaving JWT was a decision that I've never regretted, but it wasn't easy. You never know what's going to happen. All I knew at the time was that I loved writing and that I wanted to do more of it. So I kept writing and haven't stopped since. I've never been happier. And I've never been more successful.

SUZE ORMAN

Author, financial adviser and motivational speaker. Fifteen years ago, I decided that I didn't want to live a lie anymore. I wanted to stand in my truth. I didn't want people in my life that did not support me—emotionally, psychologically and spiritually. I only wanted people in my life who were positive influences on others and me. So, at the age of 50, I decided to make a clean sweep. I took a hard look at my friends, my employees and a relationship I'd been in for eight years. In just one week, I ended a lot of relationships; cutting off some friendships I'd had for a good 15 years. And I have to tell you, it was one of the best decisions I've ever made. Because the true key to success, believe it or not, is to keep good company. You might have a great idea, one that is great for you, but others will try to sabotage you. When you stand in the truth of who you are, on all levels, then you become the most powerful person that you can be. The world is attracted to truth. The world is repelled by lies. When people can feel something isn't right, they're repelled from you, from your product, from your idea, from hiring you, from being around you. When you speak the truth—and act in the truth— everybody is attracted to you.

ALANA JANE NICHOLS

Three-time gold medalist in the Paralympic Games. I went to college at the University of New Mexico. To everyone there, I was a disabled girl in a wheelchair. I got really depressed. I started thinking about suicide. I just didn't want to live the rest of my life in that chair. It was unbearable. Then I rolled into the university gym one Wednesday afternoon. That's when I saw a whole team of people playing basketball in wheelchairs. They were violent and loud and hitting each other. They'd fall over in their wheelchairs; then just get back up. It was wild and ridiculous. At some point they noticed me, and they stopped playing. They asked me my name. They asked me if I wanted to play. I had always been a rough-and-tumble girl, but since my accident, everyone had treated me like I was fragile. That day I rolled myself onto the court, and I decided to keep playing.

SETH GODIN

Author and entrepreneur. The best decision I ever made was the decision to start making decisions. To respond and initiate, not merely to react or take what's on offer. Mostly, the commitment to pick myself, to pursue a path that mattered to me and the people I work with. We have way more freedom than we realize, but it begins with deciding and choice making.

SOLEDAD O'BRIEN

Award-winning broadcast journalist and CEO of Starfish Media Group. I knew I wanted to have a substantial career. I also knew I wanted to get married and have kids. Lots of kids. Because I was very strategic about it, it helped me make decisions all along the way. I had it mapped out, the things that were all important to me—career, husband, and children. Now I've been married for more than 20 years, I have four children, and I love my work. I like to give this advice to young women: Be as intentional about planning your family life as you are about planning your career. That's what worked for me. CHOICE!

ALAN PARSONS

Songwriter, musician and record producer. Who would turn down working with Pink Floyd in their heyday? I did. Recording Pink Floyd's *The Dark Side of the Moon*, was not a very lucrative activity. I was a Staff Engineer at Abbey Road Studios on a fixed salary of 35 pounds a week. Following the album's success, I turned down a substantial full-time job offer from the band to work as their recording and live sound engineer. I was fortunate enough to soon enjoy immediate chart success as an independent music producer with a number of British and American artists. I had the creative freedom to produce artists of my own choice, and to continue with the formation of The Alan Parsons Project, which in retrospect might not have happened if I had accepted that job.

JOEL OSTEEN

Senior Pastor of Lakewood Church in Houston and author of Think Better, Live Better! My best decision, after marrying my wife, Victoria, of course, was the decision to take over as the senior pastor at Lakewood Church. After my father went to be with the Lord, I felt a deep desire to step up and serve as pastor of Lakewood Church. Having preached only once in my life—a week before my father died—that desire was soon bombarded by a variety of negative thoughts. Today when I see the opportunities to make a difference in the lives of so many people, I am truly grateful for God's grace and the strength to have made that decision years ago. IT'S A MATTER OF CHOICE!

MIKE RAWLINGS

Mayor of Dallas I've made a lot of decisions—I'm old—but I think the seminal one for me was deciding to stay in Dallas. I came to Dallas in 1976 after graduating from Boston College. I didn't like Dallas very much. I thought I'd stay here for a few years, then move back East. But I went through a divorce in my first marriage and my daughter was here. I really wanted to be near her. So I decided to stay in Dallas. And I think that made me accomplish what I think is the most important job a person has, if you're lucky enough to have kids: to be a good parent. I think how you go about decision-making is important. A lot of decisions I face, I don't immediately know what the right answers are. If I've got the time, I let those decisions come to me. You need to feel decisions as well as think them; they have to make sense both intellectually and emotionally. Then once you know what the answer is, you move quickly.

DIANE WARREN

Legendary eight-time Oscar nominee and Grammy- winning songwriter. The best decision I've ever made is to follow my own vision. I've never been someone to go around asking, "What do you think? What do you think?" I've always let my passion lead me. I've tried to just keep my blinders on and go for what I believe in. I know when something is great. When I know this, nothing stops me.

PAUL LEVINE

President of Trulia By far the best decision I ever made was to move from the East Coast to Silicon Valley 20 years ago. I grew up in the New York suburbs, and I was fascinated with technology. I realized that all of the companies I wanted to work for were located within 10 miles of each other in Silicon Valley. I wanted to be in the center of the action. I'd advise people to think about where they live, based on what they want to do. If you want to work in automotive, you might want to move to Detroit. If you're interested in entertaining, you probably want to be in Los Angeles. Get to where the action is.

Co-founder of The Huffington Post and author of "The Sleep Revolution". The best decision I ever made was committing to getting eight hours of sleep a night. For many years I subscribed to a very flawed definition of success, buying into our collective delusion that burnout is the necessary price we must pay for success. Then in 2007, I had a painful wakeup call: I fainted from sleep-deprivation and exhaustion, hit my head on my desk, and broke my cheekbone. From that point on, I knew I had to make sleep a priority. Now, 95 percent of the time I get eight hours of sleep a night. Once I started giving sleep the respect it deserves, my life improved in pretty much every way. Now, instead of waking up to the sense that I have to trudge through activities, I wake up feeling joyful about the day's possibilities. I'm also better able to recognize red flags and rebound from setbacks.

It's like being dialed into a different channel that has less static.

ED ASNER————————————————————

TV legend and winner of seven Emmy awards. The best decision I ever made was taking the job on The Mary Tyler Moore Show. It was as fine a decision as I ever made. I was branching out into an area of comedy that I hadn't perfected yet, so there was a lot to master. Taking that role changed my life. One thing that comedy did for me as an actor is that, no matter how gripping a role may be, it's not real unless you can incorporate comedy into it. It always makes a role more believable. That role helped me learn so many things I needed to know.

MEHMET OZ, M.D.,

Surgeon, author and television personality. After 31 years, I can say without question that the best decision that I ever made was marrying my wife, Lisa. I found a worthy opponent and wisely put a ring on her. She had bigger aspirations for me than were on my vision board and mastered the art of telling me what I need to hear rather than what I want to hear. She fills in the many areas where I am weak and turbo- charges my strengths. In failure, she steadies my foundation. In success, she maintains a balanced perspective.

MANDY GINSBERG

CEO for Match Group North America The night before my mother died of ovarian cancer, she did a blood test, and we discovered she had the BRCA1 mutation. With this mutation, you have a roughly 90 per cent chance of having breast cancer—which my mom had in her 30s—and you have a up to 70 per cent chance of having ovarian cancer. I got tested, and I tested positive for the defect. Then I had a choice to make. Unlike the genetic tests for Alzheimer's—for which there's not much you can do—you can take preventive measures for this. So in my 40s, I had a preventative double mastectomy, and then a couple of years later I had a hysterectomy and oophorectomy. In some ways, it wasn't even a decision—I watched my mother die. With my genetics, I felt as if a bomb were going to go off at any minute. It has given me a great sense of relief, the feeling that I will have a longer runway in front of me, more time to spend with my own two daughters, more time to do the work that I love.

LYNN WHITFIELD

Actress and producer When I was younger, several people forced me to think seriously about planning for retirement. So I did that, kicking and screaming. But now that I'm older, I'm grateful. That has allowed me to explore my art, without worrying about whether I work next week. It's given me a great deal of security and freedom. Another big decision is that three or four years ago I re-evaluated my priorities, took another look at what it takes for me to be comfortable. I started downsizing and that has made such a huge difference. I have no interest in keeping up with the Joneses or anyone else. I chose to simplify and pare down, do what I want to do, be where I want to be. I have so many friends who are very well off and they are still having conversations about not being fulfilled. They're wondering, what is the meaning of my life? I don't feel that way because I feel as if I'm living my purpose.

DAVE COULIER

Stand-up comedian and actor in the Netflix series, Fuller House, and author of "The Adventures of Jimmy Burger". I grew up in Detroit, and everyone there worked in the automotive industry. You pretty much decided between the big three: Chrysler, General Motors or Ford. But I was interested in entertainment and stand-up comedy and doing silly voices for a living. So I moved to Los Angeles and threw myself into the unknown fire. I also decided to forgo college, and everyone thought I was crazy. But I thought, no one in college is going to teach me how to do funny cartoon voices or how to be a comedy writer. Back then, at 19 years old, I was too inexperienced and naive to know the odds—they weren't good. But it ended up being the best decision I ever made because it completely shaped and changed my world.

IAN ZIERING

Actor in Beverly Hills 90210 and Sharknado, and entrepreneur. I've always looked at the celebrity I've earned as capital. I believe spending that capital doing good things for other people is the best way to spend it. When I was asked to participate in The Celebrity Apprentice, I felt lucky and honored to have the chance to raise money and awareness of a horrible disease called epidermolysis bullosa. With that goal in mind, I came to the show with a no-lose mentality, and it was the best decision I ever made. Though Leeza Gibbons ultimately won the title and $320,000 for EBKids. org, getting to mention EB on every prime time show produced that season was all I needed to feel like a winner.

KATIE KELLETT

Director of Imprints at Arcadia Publishing. At 40 years old I made a decision to run. It wasn't a well-thought-out decision; it was a spur of the moment choice on a miserably hot summer day in Charleston, South Carolina. I am the most unlikely of runners: I have never been an athlete, I smoked for the better part of two decades, and I was one of those people who always quipped, "I only run if someone is chasing me with a knife." But in the months that preceded that hot summer day, I had quit smoking and I'd begun to exercise. I was going through a divorce and looking for positive outlets to channel my anger and anxiety, wishing especially not to channel them toward my 5-year-old daughter. So I laced up my shoes, walked out the door and started to run. That first run was brutal and, truth be told, almost every one of them has been brutal since that day. And although I haven't exactly hated shopping for smaller clothes, the real reward has been something much deeper. Running has opened up ideas of possibility for me; I see myself in a different light.

SARAH HEPOLA────────────────────────

Author of the New York Times best-seller, "Blackout". I quit drinking at the age of 35. I did not want to do it. I'd loved alcohol since I was a girl. It had been my rebellion, my path to adventure, my identity, my life companion and, eventually, my undoing. What happens when you rely on booze to fix you is that you don't learn to soothe yourself. I've heard other problem drinkers say if they hadn't quit, they probably would have died. I never thought that. But I did think. If I don't quit, I'm never going to live. My world had become so small by the end. Addiction is life on a very short leash. I was unhappy—no, miserable—for the first year of sobriety. I felt bitter and robbed, but with time I began to see how much I had been drinking away: my gifts, my clarity, this present moment. Sobriety was a chance to start my life over and discover all the joys in my own body that I had been drinking in order to find: confidence, creative inspiration, pleasure. I am 41 now, a beginner in many ways, and I think of quitting drinking as the beginning of my adulthood—the moment I decided to take full responsibility for my life and, in doing so, finally made it great.

Motivational speaker and co-author of "Chicken Soup for the Soul". The best decision that I ever made after my painful divorce was to keep my heart open to the idea that I could still find my true love in this lifetime. I started by writing a list of 267 ideals that I desired in a marriage and marital partner, if I were ever to marry again. I wanted someone who could share my values, spiritual beliefs, ambition, desire, drive, hopes, and big goals for the future. I wrote that we needed to have absolute love for each other and a mutual affinity for projects we undertook. I believe that clarity of thinking and spiritual alignment with God creates the space for dreams and goals to manifest. Once created, then you need to be awake and aware when the answered prayers show up on your path. My answer presented at an Author 101 conference. From the stage, I saw in the audience a vision of loveliness, charisma, style, and perfection in motion. I asked and discovered the woman I couldn't take my eyes off was divorced. Fortuitously, in the evening VIP reception where I was surrounded by people who were barraging me with questions. I noticed from across the room, someone suddenly spilled red wine on this glorious woman's white slacks. Opportunity presented itself. I responded. I broke from my group of fans and rushed to her rescue. I promised that I knew the secret doorway to the kitchen and the Club Soda to save her stained slacks. I took her hand and rushed us out of the questioning throngs, and once the club soda was procured, I was able to chat a little bit with her to find out more about her. We had instant camaraderie and after a few minutes of chatting, I knew there was something very special about this woman, and our encounter. Even her name, Crystal, seemed like the perfect fit. I gently invited Crystal to dine at a nice restaurant in the Hollywood neighborhood, and she admitted she was starving, as was I. When we arrived at the restaurant, the line to get in was long and a hundred-dollar bill would not gain entry, I felt assured. I approached the maître d' smiling. He looked at her, saw her radiant undeniable glow and said to me: "Who is she?" I jokingly said: "She is the Queen of Denmark." He said, "No way, really?" Oh my gosh, she is! And who are you?" I know as a lifelong sales trainer to answer a question with a question and said playfully, "Who travels with the Queen?" "Oh my, you're the King! Wait right here one second and we'll get you the perfect table." I glanced at Crystal who had a huge smile on her face. She whispered, "I think it's too late to tell him you were kidding." After a couple of hours of extraordinary conversation and a lovely dinner, it felt like we had known each other forever. Throughout our courtship, I would have to pinch myself because it really seemed as though my dreams had truly been fulfilled. I asked her repeatedly to marry me because she always said "Yes!" and I never got tired of hearing that answer! Eight years later we are happily married, beyond what either of us ever imagined could have happened. It is said there is a level beyond Soul Mates, called Twin Flames in which when two people come together, like flames from two candles when they're joined, they rise together as one flame to exponentially higher levels. Crystal is my Twin Flame and I am hers. After almost giving up on love after my bitter divorce, the decision I made to find the courage to continue to believe in my dreams and goals, and in the divine power that orchestrates them into reality is the best decision I have ever or will ever make.

DR. TRAVIS STORK

ER physician, best-selling author and host of the Emmy Award-winning series, "The Doctors": I never intended to be a doctor and took a consulting job after I graduated as a math and economics major from Duke. I began volunteering at a free health clinic and it was there that I found my true calling. The best decision I ever made was to take a leap of faith and go back to medical school. I took the prerequisite classes needed at night while continuing to work. I still remember, like it was yesterday, shedding tears of joy as I sat on my front porch reading my medical school acceptance letter. My career in medicine has given my life purpose and helping people live the healthiest life possible has become my true passion.

CHAPTER 10

HOLDING ON TO YOUR CHOICE

Having discussed the importance of choice and digested the principles of choice making, I want to tackle one major issue; that is how to avoid the pressure of appeal to numbers or authority and hold unto one's own choice. One may ask what if I make the choice, but other options come afterwards? What if I'm convinced to change my choice? What if my choice doesn't work?

One of the major problems that young people have when it comes to the issues of life choices is the feeling that it may displease their guardians or friends. But let me bring to the knowledge of those with such assertion that, the repercussion of such choices does not affect any other person as much as you.

Priscilla Asamoah recounts her story. She was faced with the issue of choice pertaining to the course of study in senior high school. She chose to read Elective Mathematics because almost all her friends were offering elective mathematics. Priscilla knows very well that she faces a lot of difficulties when it comes to mathematics but in as much as her friends would do mathematics, she has to be in class with them and that meaning her choosing mathematics. Unfortunate right?

It is also common for parents to choose certain schools and courses and specific programs for their wards. This is done without taking into consideration the interests, strengths and weaknesses of the child. Some families practically arrange the school, programs to pursue in high schools, academic qualifications, professional and career choices for a child yet unborn. Some go to the extent of writing those fantasies and erroneous beliefs down for reference. They end up either being disappointed or enforcing those daydreams and wild wishes upon the innocent children who may be born with other natural talents and gifts that do conform to their own viewpoint. They forget that these natural gifts and talents could propel the child to achieve exploits with joy, ease and without stress.

That, unfortunately, is the story of many young people who are faced with the situation of choice making, be it in the educational field, courses of study, life partners, career, religion and even business decisions.

The individual who wants to be happy in life must appreciate the might of choices and understand that choices make and unmake great men. He must be quick to recognize the wrong choices made in the past and hasten to adopt the right ones that can help him achieve the desired success and fulfillment.

Your life, your choices. Your choices today will determine your future. Make the right choice today.

APPENDIX

One of the prerequisites to achieving one's career goal is to have the appropriate orientation and information about the field. It is to be noted that, what an individual wishes to achieve does not fully rely or depend on the early stages of studies as per the educational system in our part of the world. In some cases, it only builds one's confidence in a particular field and introduces the individual to the possibilities of continuing the dream to major in a career of interest or to change option. TRUE EDUCATION is the soundest investment you can make in yourself! But, let's be sure we understand what Education really is. Some folks measure Education by the number of years spent in school or the number of certificates, diplomas or degrees earned. This quantitative approach to Education does not necessarily produce a successful person. We are interested in competency, not diplomas". A diploma or degree may help you get a job, but it will not guarantee your progress on the job. "Business is interested in competency, not diplomas."

To others, Education means the quality of information a person has stashed away in his brain. But the soak-up-facts method of Education won't get you where you want to go. More and more people depend on books, files and machines to warehouse information. If this is so we can do only what a machine can do, then we are in a real fix!

Real Education, the kind worth investing in, is that which develops and cultivates your mind. How well educated a person is, is measured by how well his mind is developed. In brief, by how well he thinks.

Anything that improves thinking ability is Education. We can obtain Education in many ways. The most efficient sources of Education for most people are nearby colleges and universities. To them, Education is business!

If you haven't been to college lately, you're in for some wonderful surprises. You'll be pleased at the wide course offerings available. You'll be even more pleased to discover who goes to school after work. Not the phonies, but rather really promising persons, many of who already hold very responsible positions. In one evening class of twenty-five persons I conducted recently, there were an owner of a retail chain of twelve stores, two buyers for a national food chain, four graduate engineers, an Air Force Captain, and several others of similar status!

Many people earn degrees in evening programs these days, but the degree, which in the final analysis is only a piece of paper, is not their primary motivation. They are going to school to build their minds, which is a sure way to invest in a better future.

And make no mistakes about this. Education is a real bargain. A moderate investment will keep you in school one night each week for a full year. Compute the cost as a percentage of your gross income and then ask yourself, "Isn't my future worth a small investment?"

Why not make an investment decision right now? Call it "School: One Night a Week for Life". It will keep you abreast of your areas of interest. And it will surround you with other people who are also going places!

Invest in idea starters. Education helps you mould your mind, stretch it, train it to meet new situations and solve problems. Idea starters serve a related purpose. They feed your mind, and give you constructive material to think about.

Where are the best sources of idea starters? There are many, but to get a steady supply of high-quality idea material, why not do this: Resolve to purchase at least one stimulating book each month, but subscribe to two magazines or journals that stress ideas. For only a minor sum and a minimum of time, you can be tuned in to some of the best thinkers available anywhere.

At a luncheon one day, I overheard one fellow say, "But it costs too much. I can't afford to take The Wall Street Journal". His companion, obviously a much more success-minded person, replied, "Well, I've found that I can't afford not to take it".

Again, take your cue from successful people. Invest in yourself!

One of the major moments of choice making in an individual's life, and where many get confused with others losing it, is that stage after high school where one is faced with the challenge of choosing a tertiary school for further studies and the courses available to them in such institutions.

Note that, this is a critical aspect where your own specialties should be taken into serious consideration. The type of school will affect your performance, the choice of course to study and the location of the school are all factors that should be considered. Some may want to attend schools that are close to home and others may prefer schools far away. In these choices just make sure that you are deciding based on positive agenda and the desire to succeed. Never make that mistake. Recognise yourself and what you want, and it shall work well for you. Never make a choice all because your friends have made that option a priority.

Below are the lists of various tertiary institutions we have in Ghana. I hope that it guides you to make the right choices in the area of education.

LIST OF UNIVERSITIES IN GHANA

This is a list of Universities in Ghana. For the purposes of this list, Colleges and universities are defined as accredited, degree-granting, polytechnic institutions. Small Universities are, merged and incorporated as affiliated institutions into larger institutions, and most higher education institutions are named "University College". The country's Colleges which are incorporated with universities are listed as "University College". The country's "polytechnics" are also listed.

There are other educational institutions in Ghana some are local campuses of foreign Universities, some conduct classes for students who write their exams at the distance education centers of the larger Ghanaian Universities. Universities and colleges are accredited by the National Accreditation Board Ghana, under the Ministry of Education Ghana.

S/No	Institution	Nickname	Founded	Location(s)
1.	University of Ghana	Legon	1948	Legon, Accra, Korle Bu and Atomic, Greater Accra Region, including over ten Workers' Colleges all over the ten regions of Ghana as at 20
2.	Kwame Nkrumah University of Science and Technology	KNUST	1952	Kumasi, Ashanti Region
3.	University of Cape Coast	Cape Vars	1961	Cape Coast, Central Region
4.	University of Education, Winneba	UEW	1992	Winneba, Central Region
5.	University for Development Studies	UDS	1992	Tamale, Northern Region
6.	University of Professional Studies	UPS	1965	Accra, Greater Accra Region

S/No	Institution	Nickname	Founded	Location(s)
7.	University of Mines and Technology	UMAT	2001	Tarkwa, Western Region
8.	University of Health and Allied Sciences	UHAS	2011	Ho, Volta Region
9.	University Of Energy and Natural Resources	UENR	2012	Sunyani, Brong Ahafo Region
10.	Accra Technical University	ATU		Accra, Greater Accra Region
11.	Cape Coast Technical University	CCTU		Cape Coast, Central Region
12.	Kumasi Technical University	KsTU		Kumasi, Ashanti Region
13.	Koforidua Technical University	KTU		Koforidua, Eastern Region
14.	Tamale Technical University	TATU		Tamale, Northern Region
15.	Ho Technical University	HTU		Ho, Volta Region
16.	Takoradi Technical University	TTU		Takoradi, Western Region

 Power of Choice

S/No	Institution	Nickname	Founded	Location(s)
17.	Sunyani Technical University	STU		Sunyani, Brong Ahafo Region
18.	Ghana Armed Forces Command and Staff College	GAFCSC		Accra, Greater Accra Region
19.	Ghana Institute of Journalism	GIJ		Accra, Greater Accra Region (formerly affiliated to the University of Ghana)
20.	Ghana Institute of Languages	GIL	1961	Accra, Greater Accra Region (affiliated to the University of Ghana)
21.	Ghana Institute of Management and Public Administration	GIMPA		Legon, Greater Accra Region (formerly affiliated to the University of Ghana)

S/No	Institution	Nickname	Founded	Location(s)
22.	Ghana Institute of Surveying and Mapping	GISM		Accra, Greater Accra Region
23.	Institution of Local Government Studies	ILGS		Legon, Greater Accra Region
24.	Kofi Annan International Peacekeeping Training Centre[2]	KAIPTC	1998	Accra, Greater Accra Region
25.	National Film and Television Institute	NAFTI	1978	Accra, Greater Accra Region
26.	Regional Maritime University[4]	RMU	2007	Accra, Greater Accra Region
27.	Consular & Diplomatic Service University (CDSU)[5]	CDSU	2017	Accra, Greater Accra Region
28.	Valley View University	VVU	1979	Oyibi, Greater Accra Region
29.	Akrofi Christaller Institute of Theology, Mission and Culture Communications	ACI	1987	Akropong–Akuapem, Eastern Region
30.	Accra Institute of Technology	AIT	2005	Cantonments, Greater Accra Region

S/No	Institution	Nickname	Founded	Location(s)
31.	African University College of Communication	AUCC		Adabraka, Greater Accra Region, Ghana
32.	Anglican University College of Technology	ANG.U.TECH	2008	Nkoranza Campus, Nkoranza, Brong Ahafo Region
33.	Catholic University College of Ghana	CUG	2003	Fiapre, Sunyani, Brong Ahafo Region
34.	Christian Service University College	CSUC	1974	Kumasi, Ashanti Region
35.	Family Health Medical School	FHMS	2015	Teshie, Greater Accra Region
36.	Good News Theological Seminary	GNTS	1971	Oyibi, Greater Accra Region
37.	Islamic University College[6]	ICUG	1988	East Legon, Greater Accra Region
38.	Knutsford University College	Knutsford		East Legon, Greater Accra Region
39.	Lancaster University	LUG	2013	Accra, Greater Accra Region

S/No	Institution	Nickname	Founded	Location(s)
40.	Methodist University College Ghana[6]	MUCG	2000	Dansoman, Accra, Greater Accra Region
41.	Pentecost University College[6]	Pent Vars	2003	Sowutuom, Greater Accra Region
42.	Presbyterian University College[7]	PUC	2003	Abetifi-Kwahu, Akropong-Akuapem, Agogo Asante-Akyem and Tema
43.	Catholic Institute of Business and Technology	CIBT		Accra, Greater Accra Region
44.	Institute of Accountancy Training	IAT		Accra, Greater Accra Region
45.	Narh-Bita School of Nursing	Narh-Bita		Accra, Greater Accra Region
46.	St. Victor's Seminary	SVMS		Accra, Greater Accra Region
47.	St. Peters Seminary	SPMS		Accra, Greater Accra Region
48.	St. Paul Seminary	SPCS		Accra, Greater Accra Region

S/No	Institution	Nickname	Founded	Location(s)
49.	Blue Crest College (formerly NIIT Ghana College)	BCCG	1999	Accra, Greater Accra Region (affiliated to the University of Education, Winneba)
50.	Osei Tutu II Institute for Advanced ICT Studies			Kumasi, Ashanti Region
51.	KAAF University College	KUC		Gomoa Buduburam, Central Region
52.	All Nations University College[7]	ANUC	2002	Koforidua, Eastern Region (affiliated to the Kwame Nkrumah University of Science & Technology)
53.	Radford University College	Radford		Kumasi, Ashanti Region
54.	Garden City University College[7]	GCUC	2001	Kumasi, Ashanti Region

S/No	Institution	Nickname	Founded	Location(s)
55.	Regent University College of Science and Technology[7]	Regent	2003	Accra, Greater Accra Region (affiliated to the Maastricht School of Management, Netherlands)
56.	Technical University College	TUC		Tamale, Northern Region (affiliated to the University of Ghana)
57.	Spiritan University College	Spiritan		Ejisu, Ashanti Region
58.	Data Link University College	DLUC	2006	Tema, Greater Accra Region
59.	Mountcrest University College	MCUC		Kanda, Accra, Greater Accra Region
60.	University College of Agriculture and Environmental Studies	UCAES	1963	Bunso, Eastern Region

 Power of Choice

S/No	Institution	Nickname	Founded	Location(s)
61.	Central University College	Central	1998	Accra, Greater Accra Region (affiliated to the University of Cape Coast)
62.	Ashesi University[7]	Ashesi	2002	Accra, Greater Accra Region
63.	Entrepreneurshi p Training Institute	ETI		Accra, Greater Accra Region
64.	Deltas University College	DUC		Accra, Greater Accra Region
65.	Evangelical Presbyterian University College	EPUC	2008	Ho, Volta Region
66.	Ghana Baptist University College [7]	GBUC	2006	Abuakwa kumasi, Ashanti Region
67.	Kings University College	KUC		Aplaku Hills, Accra, Greater Accra Region
68.	Maranatha University College	MUC		Sowutuom, Accra, Greater Accra Region

S/No	Institution	Nickname	Founded	Location(s)
69.	Meridian (Insaaniyya) University College[7]	MEDUCOL		Weija, Accra, Greater Accra Region
70.	Pan African Christian University College	PACUC		Accra, Greater Accra Region (affiliation under negotiation)
71.	Wisconsin International University College[6]	WIUC	2000	Agbogba Junction, Greater Accra Region (also affiliated to the University of Ghana)
72.	Advanced Business University College	ABUC		Accra, Greater Accra Region
73.	BlueCrest University College[8]	BCUC	2000	Accra, Greater Accra Region, Kumasi, Ashanti Region
74.	Jayee University College	JUC		Accra, Greater Accra Region

 Power of Choice

S/No	Institution	Nickname	Founded	Location(s)
75.	University College of Management Studies	UCOMS	1974	Accra, Greater Accra Region, Kumasi, Ashanti Region
76.	Webster University Ghana Campus	Webster	2012	Luanda Close, East Legon, Accra, Greater Accra Region
77.	Sikkim Manipal University Ghana LC	SMUG	2008	Academic City, Ring Road, Accra, Greater Accra Region
78.	Sikkim Manipal University, Kumasi	SMUG	2011	CityStyle Building, Stadium Road, Kumasi, Ashanti Region
79.	Ghana Christian University College	GCUC		Accra, Greater Accra Region, Kumasi, Ashanti Region (affiliation under negotiation)

S/No	Institution	Nickname	Founded	Location(s)
80.	Zenith University College[7]	ZUC	2001	La, Accra, Greater Accra Region, Kumasi, Ashanti Region (affiliated to the University of Cape Coast)
81.	China Europe International Business School	CEIBS	1994	Accra, Greater Accra Region
82.	Ghana Christian University College	GCUC		Dodowa, Accra, Greater Accra Region
83.	The Bible University College of Ghana	BUCG		Akuapem, Eastern Region
84.	Catholic Institute of Business and Technology	CIBT		Accra, Greater Accra Region
85.	Ghana Telecom University College	GTUC	2005	Tesano, Accra, Greater Accra Region

| 86. | North American Center for Professional Studies | NACPS | 2011 | Kasoa, Central Region |
| 87. | Premier Institute of Law Enforcement Management and Administration | PILEMA | | Accra, Greater Accra Region |

COLLEGES OF EDUCATION IN GHANA
(TEACHER TRAINING COLLEGES)

The Colleges of Education are responsible for Teacher Education. A further two private Colleges are to be absorbed into the group of 41 public institutions, raising the number to 43. This is a list of the Colleges of Education in Ghana (including those that were absorbed recently):

S/No	Institution	Tel. No	Address
1.	Abetifi Presbyterian College of Education	0342030177	P. O. Box 19, Abetifi
2.	Accra College of Education	0302865737	P. O. Box 221, Legon
3.	Ada College of Education	0303522220	P. O. Box 34, Ada
4.	Agogo Presbyterian College of Education	0322092185	P. O. Box 26, Agogo
5.	Akatsi College of Education	0362644408	P. O. Box Pmb, Akatsiakatsico@ Yahoo.Com
6.	Akrokerri College of Education	0322021659	P. O. Box 32, Akrokerri
7.	Atebubu College of Education	0352622024	P. O. Box 29, Atebubu
8.	Bagabaga College of Education	0372023247	P. O. Box 35, Tamale
9.	Berekum College of Education	0352222018	P. O. Box 74, Berekum
10.	Bimbila E.P. College of Education	0372023742 0372023180	P. O. Box 16, Bimbila

S/No	Institution	Tel. No	Address
11.	Dambai College of Education	0362122103	P. O. Box 84, Dambai
12.	Enchi College of Education		Enchi
13.	Evangelical Presbyterian College of Education	0362122002 0362122009	P. O. Box 12, Amedzofe
14.	Foso College of Education		P. O. Box Pmb, Foso
15.	Gbewaa College of Education		P. O. Box 157, Bawku
16.	Holy Child College of Education	0312023430	P. O. Box 245, Takoradi
17.	Jasikan College of Education		P. O. Box 14, Jasikan
18.	Kibi Presbyterian College of Education	0342030766	P. O. Box Pmb, Kibi
19.	Komenda College of Education	0312095131	P. O. Box Km5, Komenda
20.	Mampong Technical College of Education	0322222209	P. O. Box 31, Mampong- Ashanti
21.	Mount Mary College of Education	0342091414	P. O. Box 19, Somanya
22.	Nusrat Jahan College of Education	0392022338	P. O. Box 71, Wa
23.	Ofinso College of Education		P. O. Box 7, Offinso-Ashanti
24.	Ola College of Education	0332133256 0332133202	P. O. Box 175, Cape Coast

S/No	Institution	Tel. No	Address
25.	Peki College of Education	0362722043	P. O. Box 14, Peki
26.	Presbyterian College of Education	0342722199	P. O. Box 27, Akropong-Akuapem
27.	Presbyterian Women's College of Education	0342822039	P. O. Box 19, Aburi
28.	SDA College of Education	0342021281	P. O. Box 18, Asokore- Koforidua
29.	St John Bosco College of Education	0382122617	P. O. Box 11, Navrongo
30.	St. Francis' College of Education	0362722006	P. O. Box 100, Hohoe
31.	St. Joseph College of Education	0352122332	P. O. Box 15, Bechem
32.	St. Louis College of Education	0322028081	P. O. Box 3041, Kumasi
33.	St. Monica's College of Education	0322222205	P. O. Box 250, Mampong- Ashanti
34.	St. Teresa's College of Education	0362722043	P. O. Box 129, Hohoe
35.	Tamale College of Education	0372023687	P. O. Box 14, Tamale
36.	Tumu College of Education	0392020901	P. O. Box 19, Tumu
37.	Wesley College of Education	0322028541 0322022264	P. O. Box 1927, Kumasi

S/No	Institution	Tel. No	Address
38.	Wiawso College of Education	0312095131	P. O. Box 945, Wiawso
39.	Aim Professionals Institute and Training College	0362091581 0277854465	P. O. Box Hp 1289, Ho
40.	Cambridge Teacher Training College		Website: Www.Cambridge college.Co.Uk
41.	Holy Spirit College of Education	0362027114	P. O. Box Hp 1196, Ho
42.	Jackson College of Education	0208163911	P. O. Box Up 950, Knust – Kumasi
43.	Mccoy College of Education Principal		C/O Catholic Secretariat P. O. Box 47, Nadowli-Wa
44.	Methodist College of Education		Akim Oda
45.	Sda College of Education		P. O. Box 480 , Agona-Kuamsi
46.	St Ambrose College of Education		Dromaa Akwamu, B/A
47.	Al-Faruq College of Education		Wenchi/Droboso
48.	Bia Lamplighter College of Education		Sefwi-Debiso
49.	Gambaga College of Education		Gambaga
50.	Our Lady of Apostles (Ola) College of Education		Cape Coast

LIST OF APPROVED NURSING AND MIDWIFERY TRAINING INSTITUTIONS AND PROGRAMMES
GREATER ACCRA REGION

NO.	NAME OF SCHOOL	PROGRAMME												POST NAC/NAP MIDWIFERY	OWNERSHIP	
		BASIC				AUXILIARIES		POST BASIC NURSING							STATE	PRIVATE
		RGN	RCN	RMN	RM	NAP	NAC	CCN	PON	ENT	PHN	OPN	PN	MID		
1.	University of Ghana, Legon, Accra	✓ *											*		✓	
2.	Valley View University, Oyibi, Accra	✓ *														✓
3.	Central University College, Miotso	✓ *														✓
4.	St. Karol Sch. of Nursing, Weija, Accra	✓ *														✓
5.	Pentecost University College, Sowutuom Accra	✓ *														✓
6.	West End University College, Weija Accra	✓ *														✓
7.	Nursing & Midwifery Training School , Korle-Bu, Accra	✓			✓										✓	

No.	Institution															
8.	Nursing & Midwifery Training School, 37 Military, Accra.	✓			✓		#								✓	
9.	Western Hills School of Nursing, Accra.	✓					✓									✓
10.	Nightingale School of Nursing, Accra.	✓														✓
11.	Narh Bita College , Tema	✓					✓							✓		✓
12.	Nurses Training College, Pantang.			✓											✓	
13.	Nursing & Midwifery Training College, Pantang.				✓		✓							✓	✓	
14.	Nursing & Midwifery Training College, Teshie.	✓			✓		✓							✓	✓	

BASIC PROGRAMMES

RGN - Registered General Nursing

RMN - Registered Mental Nursing

RCN - Registered Community Nursing

RM   - Registered Midwifery

OTHER KEYS

*   - Bachelor of Science (BSc)

- Training Curtailed

AUXILIARY PROGRAMMES

NAP - Nurse Assistant (Preventive)

NAC - Nurse Assistant (Clinical)

POST AUXILIAY MIDWIFERY

MID -Post NAC/NAP Midwifery

EN - Emergency Nursing

POST BASIC NURSING (PROGRAMMES)

OPN - Ophthalmic Nursing

CCN - Critical Care Nursing

PON - Peri-Operative Nursing

PHN - Public Hmjealth Nursing

ENT - Ear Nose & Throat Nursing

PN - Paediatric Nursing

S/No	NAME OF SCHOOL	RGN	RCN	RMN	RM	NAP	NAC	CCN	PON	ENT	PHN	OPN	PN	MID	OWNERSHIP	
															STATE	PRIVATE
15.	Martin Luther Health Training School,						✓									✓
16.	Family Health University College School of Nursing and Midwifery, Teshie-Nungua, Accra	✓			✓		✓									✓
17.	Health Concern Ghana, Accra						✓									✓
18.	Nyaniba Health Assistant Training School, Tema						✓									✓
19.	Ophthalmic Nursing School, Korle-Bu											✓			✓	
20.	Critical Care Nursing & Peri Operative Nursing School							✓	✓						✓	
21.	Public Health Nurses Training School, Korle-Bu		✓								✓				✓	

22.	Golden Sunbeam International College of Science and Technology, Ayikuma-Accra	✓ *														✓
23.	Ghana Christian University College, Adenta-Accra	✓ *														✓
24.	Wisconsin International University College, Accra	✓ *	✓ *		✓ *											✓
25.	Oak City International College Madina-Accra	✓ *														✓
	TOTAL	18	2	1	6	-	6	1	1	-	1	1	0	3	9	16

BASIC PROGRAMMES

RGN - Registered General Nursing

RMN - Registered Mental Nursing

RCN - Registered Community Nursing

RM   - Registered Midwifery

OTHER KEYS

*   - Bachelor of Science (BSc)

- Training Curtailed

AUXILIARY PROGRAMMES

NAP - Nurse Assistant (Preventive)

NAC - Nurse Assistant (Clinical)

POST AUXILIAY MIDWIFERY

MID -Post NAC/NAP Midwifery

EN - Emergency Nursing

POST BASIC NURSING (PROGRAMMES)

OPN - Ophthalmic Nursing

CCN - Critical care Nursing

PON - Peri-Operative Nursing

PHN - Public health Nursing

ENT - Ear Nose & Throat Nursing

PN - Paediatric Nursing

LIST OF APPROVED NURSING AND MIDWIFERY TRAINING INSTITUTIONS AND PROGRAMMES
ASHANTI REGION

NO.	NAME OF SCHOOL	PROGRAMME														OWNERSHIP	
		BASIC				AUXILIARIES		POST BASIC NURSING							POST NAC/NAP MIDWIFERY	STATE	PRIVATE
		RGN	RCN	RMN	RM	NAP	NAC	CCN	PON	ENT	PHN	OPN	PN	EMN	MID		
1.	KNUST, Kumasi	✓ *			✓											✓	
2.	Presby University College ,Agogo	✓															✓
3.	Christian Service University College ,Kumasi	✓															✓
4.	Garden City University College, Kumasi (Dip. & BSc)	✓			✓												✓
5.	Presby Nursing and Midwifery Training College , Agogo	✓													✓	✓	

No.	Institution														
6.	Nursing & Midwifery Training College , Kumasi	✓		✓										✓	
7.	SDA Nurses Training College , Kwadaso	✓												✓	
8.	Premier School of Nursing, Moshie Zongo, Kumasi	✓				✓									✓
9.	Nursing and Midwifery Training College, Ashanti Mampong	✓		✓		✓						✓		✓	
10.	Nursing and Midwifery Training College, Maase Offinso	✓		✓										✓	

No.	Institution															
11.	Midwifery Training School Jaachi Pramso				✓									✓	✓	
12.	Samlee Nursing and Midwifery Training College, Kumasi						✓						✓	✓		
13.	Community Health Nurses Training School Fomena		✓			✓								✓	✓	
14.	Nurses Training College, Kokofu	✓													✓	
15.	Nursing and Midwifery Training College, Tepa	✓			✓		✓								✓	
16.	ENT Nurses Training School, Kumasi										✓				✓	

No.	Institution														
17.	Abot College of Health Sciences and Technology, Kumasi	✓													✓
18.	College of Integrated Healthcare, Obuasi			✓											✓
19.	Ghana Baptist University College, Kumasi	✓ *													✓
20.	Royal Ann College Of Health, Kumasi	✓		✓											✓
21.	SDA Midwifery Training College, Asamang											✓	✓		
22.	Neumann College, Kumasi	✓ *													✓
23.	Withrow College	✓													✓

24.	Manaata School of Midwifery, Kumasi				✓											✓
	TOTAL	17	1	-	10	1	4	-	-	0	-	-	-	-	6	11	13

BASIC PROGRAMMES

RGN - Registered General Nursing

RMN - Registered Mental Nursing

RCN - Registered Community Nursing

RM   - Registered Midwifery

OTHER KEYS

* - Bachelor of Science (BSc)

- Training Curtailed

AUXILIARY PROGRAMMES

NAP - Nurse Assistant (Preventive)

NAC - Nurse Assistant (Clinical)

POST AUXILIAY MIDWIFERY

MID -Post NAC/NAP Midwifery

EN - Emergency Nursing

POST BASIC NURSING (PROGRAMMES)

OPN - Ophthalmic Nursing

CCN - Critical care Nursing

PON - Peri-Operative Nursing

PHN - Public health Nursing

ENT - Ear Nose & Throat Nursing

PN - Paediatric Nursing

LIST OF APPROVED NURSING AND MIDWIFERY TRAINING INSTITUTIONS AND PROGRAMMES
BRONG AHAFO REGION

NO.	NAME OF SCHOOL	PROGRAMME													OWNERSHIP	
		BASIC				AUXILIARIES		POST BASIC NURSING						POST NAC/NAP MIDWIFERY	STATE	PRIVATE
		RGN	RCN	RMN	RM	NAP	NAC	CCN	PON	ENT	PHN	OPN	PN			
1.	Methodist University College, Wenchi (DIP.)	✓														✓
2.	Catholic University College ,Fiapre	✓ *														✓
3.	Nursing and Midwifery Training College, Sunyani	✓			✓		✓								✓	
4.	Holy Family Nursing and Midwifery Training College , Berekum	✓			✓									✓	✓	
5.	Midwifery Training School, Dormaa Ahenkro				✓									✓	✓	

No.	Institution																
6.	Midwifery Training School, Goaso			✓										✓	✓		
7.	Community Health Nurses Training School, Tanoso		✓		✓										✓		
8.	Nurses Training College, Techiman Krobo	✓			✓										✓		
9.	Nurses Training College, Seikwa	✓				✓									✓		
10.	College of Nursing, Ntotroso	✓													✓		
11.	Holy Family NMTC, Kenten, Techiman	✓			✓										✓		
12.	Anglican University College of Technology, Nkoranza	✓ *			✓												✓
13.	Nurses' Training College, Sampa	✓													✓		
14.	Nursing Training College, Kwapong					✓									✓		

No.	Institution															
15.	Nursing and Midwifery Training College, Dadie-soaba						✓								✓	
16.	Presbyterian Midwifery Training College, Duayaw-Nkwanta				✓										✓	
	TOTAL	**10**	**1**	-	**7**	**2**	**4**	-	-	-	-	-	-	**3**	**13**	**3**

BASIC PROGRAMMES

RGN - Registered General Nursing

RMN - Registered Mental Nursing

RCN - Registered Community Nursing

RM   - Registered Midwifery

OTHER KEYS

*   - Bachelor of Science (BSc)

\#   - Training Curtailed

AUXILIARY PROGRAMMES

NAP - Nurse Assistant (Preventive)

NAC - Nurse Assistant (Clinical)

POST AUXILIAY MIDWIFERY

MID -Post NAC/NAP Midwifery

EN - Emergency Nursing

POST BASIC NURSING (PROGRAMMES)

OPN - Ophthalmic Nursing

CCN - Critical care Nursing

PON - Peri-Operative Nursing

PHN - Public health Nursing

ENT - Ear Nose & Throat Nursing

PN - Paediatric Nursing

LIST OF APPROVED NURSING AND MIDWIFERY TRAINING INSTITUTIONS AND PROGRAMMES
EASTERN REGION

NO.	NAME OF SCHOOL	PROGRAMME													OWNERSHIP	
		BASIC				AUXILIARIES		POST BASIC NURSING						POST NAC/NAP MIDWIFERY	STATE	PRIVATE
		RGN	RCN	RMN	RM	NAP	NAC	CCN	PON	ENT	PHN	OPN	PN	MID		
1.	Nursing and Midwifery Training College, Koforidua	✓			✓										✓	
2.	Holy Family Nurses Training College, Nkawkaw	✓													✓	
3.	Nursing and Midwifery Training School, Atibie	✓			✓		#							✓	✓	
4.	Community Health Nurses Training School, Akim Oda		✓			✓									✓	
5.	Nurses Training College, Osiem						✓								✓	

#	Institution															
6.	Nursing and Midwifery Training College, Afosu						✓							✓		✓
7.	VRA College of Nursing, Akosombo	✓														✓
8.	Hopkins Health Training Institute, Akim Oda	✓														✓
9.	Nursing and Midwifery Training College, Odumase- Krobo					✓									✓	
	TOTAL	5	1	-	2	2	2	-	-	-	-	-	-	2	6	3

BASIC PROGRAMMES

RGN - Registered General Nursing

RMN - Registered Mental Nursing

RCN - Registered Community Nursing

RM - Registered Midwifery

OTHER KEYS

* - Bachelor of Science (BSc)

\# - Training Curtailed

AUXILIARY PROGRAMMES

NAP - Nurse Assistant (Preventive)

NAC - Nurse Assistant (Clinical)

POST AUXILIAY MIDWIFERY

MID -Post NAC/NAP Midwifery

EN - Emergency Nursing

POST BASIC NURSING (PROGRAMMES)

OPN - Ophthalmic Nursing

CCN - Critical care Nursing

PON - Peri-Operative Nursing

PHN - Public health Nursing

ENT - Ear Nose & Throat Nursing

PN - Paediatric Nursing

LIST OF APPROVED NURSING AND MIDWIFERY TRAINING INSTITUTIONS AND PROGRAMMES
VOLTA REGION

NO.	NAME OF SCHOOL	PROGRAMME												OWNERSHIP	
		BASIC				AUXILIARIES		POST BASIC NURSING					POST NAC/NAP MIDWIFERY	STATE	PRIVATE
		RGN	RCN	RMN	RM	NAP	NAC	CCN	PON	PHN	OPN	PN	MID		
1.	University of Health & Allied Sciences, Ho	✓ *	✓ *		✓ *									✓	
2.	Nurses Training College, Ho	✓	✓			✓								✓	
3.	Midwifery Training School, Hohoe				✓									✓	
4.	Midwifery Training School, Kete Krachi				✓		✓						✓	✓	
5.	Nurses Training College, Keta	✓					#							✓	
6.	Modal College, Sogakope (Dip. & BSc)	✓ *													✓
	TOTAL	4	2	-	3	1	1	-	-	-	-	-	1	5	1

BASIC PROGRAMMES

RGN - Registered General Nursing

RMN - Registered Mental Nursing

RCN - Registered Community Nursing

RM   - Registered Midwifery

OTHER KEYS

* - Bachelor of Science (BSc)

- Training Curtailed

AUXILIARY PROGRAMMES

NAP - Nurse Assistant (Preventive)

NAC - Nurse Assistant (Clinical)

POST AUXILIAY MIDWIFERY

MID - Post NAC/NAP Midwifery

EN - Emergency Nursing

POST BASIC NURSING (PROGRAMMES)

OPN - Ophthalmic Nursing

CCN - Critical care Nursing

PON - Peri-Operative Nursing

PHN - Public health Nursing

ENT - Ear Nose & Throat Nursing

PN - Paediatric Nursing

LIST OF APPROVED NURSING AND MIDWIFERY TRAINING INSTITUTIONS AND PROGRAMMES
CENTRAL REGION

NO.	NAME OF SCHOOL	PROGRAMME												POST NAC/NAP MIDWIFERY	OWNERSHIP	
		BASIC				AUXILIARIES		POST BASIC NURSING								
		RGN	RCN	RMN	RM	NAP	NAC	CCN	PON	ENT	PHN	OPN	PN	MID	STATE	PRIVATE
1.	University of Cape Coast	✓ *													✓	
2.	KAAF University College, Kasoa	✓ *														✓
3.	Nursing and Midwifery Training College Cape Coast	✓			✓									✓	✓	
4.	Nurses Training College, Ankaful, Cape Coast			✓											✓	
5.	Community Health Nurses Training College, Winneba		✓			✓									✓	
6.	Nursing and Midwifery Training College, Twifo Praso	✓	✓		✓		✓								✓	

No.	Institution															
7.	Nursing and Midwifery Training College, Dunkwa - On- Offin	✓			✓		✓							✓	✓	
8.	BIMAKS College of Business and Health Sciences, Agona Swedru	✓			✓											✓
9.	Godfery Memorial Midwifery Training School, Apam													✓		✓
	TOTAL	6	2	1	4	1	2	-	-	-	-	-	-	3	6	3

BASIC PROGRAMMES

RGN - Registered General Nursing

RMN - Registered Mental Nursing

RCN - Registered Community Nursing

RM - Registered Midwifery

OTHER KEYS

* - Bachelor of Science (BSc)

\# - Training Curtailed

AUXILIARY PROGRAMMES

NAP - Nurse Assistant (Preventive)

NAC - Nurse Assistant (Clinical)

POST AUXILIAY MIDWIFERY

MID -Post NAC/NAP Midwifery

EN - Emergency Nursing

POST BASIC NURSING (PROGRAMMES)

OPN - Ophthalmic Nursing

CCN - Critical care Nursing

PON - Peri-Operative Nursing

PHN - Public health Nursing

ENT - Ear Nose & Throat Nursing

PN - Paediatric Nursing

LIST OF APPROVED NURSING AND MIDWIFERY TRAINING INSTITUTIONS AND PROGRAMMES
WESTERN REGION

NO.	NAME OF SCHOOL	PROGRAMME													OWNERSHIP	
		BASIC				AUXILIARIES		POST BASIC NURSING						POST NAC/NAP MIDWIERY	STATE	PRIVATE
		RGN	RCN	RMN	RM	NAP	NAC	CCN	PON	ENT	PHN	OPN	PN	MID		
1.	Nursing and Midwifery Training College Sekondi	✓			✓										✓	
2.	Midwifery Training School, Tarkwa				✓										✓	
3.	Nursing and Midwifery Training College, Asakrangwa	✓			✓		✓							✓	✓	
4.	Community Health Nurses Training College, Esiama		✓			✓									✓	
5.	Nursing and Midwifery Training College, Sefwi Wiawso	✓					✓								✓	

6.	Nursing and Midwifery Training College, Asanta	✓					✓							✓	✓	
7.	St John of God Nursing Training College, Sefwi Asafo	✓													✓	
	TOTAL	**5**	**1**	**-**	**3**	**1**	**3**	**-**	**-**	**-**	**-**	**-**	**-**	**2**	**7**	**0**

BASIC PROGRAMMES

RGN - Registered General Nursing

RMN - Registered Mental Nursing

RCN - Registered Community Nursing

RM   - Registered Midwifery

OTHER KEYS

*   - Bachelor of Science (BSc)

- Training Curtailed

AUXILIARY PROGRAMMES

NAP - Nurse Assistant (Preventive)

NAC - Nurse Assistant (Clinical)

POST AUXILIAY MIDWIFERY

MID -Post NAC/NAP Midwifery

EN - Emergency Nursing

POST BASIC NURSING (PROGRAMMES)

OPN - Ophthalmic Nursing

CCN - Critical care Nursing

PON - Peri-Operative Nursing

PHN - Public health Nursing

ENT - Ear Nose & Throat Nursing

PN - Paediatric Nursing

LIST OF APPROVED NURSING AND MIDWIFERY TRAINING INSTITUTIONS AND PROGRAMMES
NORTHERN REGION

NO.	NAME OF SCHOOL	BASIC				AUXILIARIES		POST BASIC NURSING							POST NAC/NAP MIDWIFERY	OWNERSHIP	
		RGN	RCN	RMN	RM	NAP	NAC	CCN	PON	ENT	PHN	OPN	EMN	PN	MID	STATE	PRIVATE
1.	University for Development Studies, Tamale	✓ *			✓ *											✓	
2.	Nursing and Midwifery Training School, Tamale	✓			✓											✓	
3.	Community Health Nurses Training School, Tamale		✓			✓										✓	
4.	Community Health Nurses Training School, Bole		✓			✓									✓	✓	
5.	Midwifery Training School, Gushegu				✓										✓	✓	
6.	Nursing and Midwifery Training College, Kpembe	✓			✓		✓								✓	✓	

No.	College																
7.	Nursing and Midwifery Training College, Yendi	✓		✓			✓								✓	
8.	Nursing and Midwifery Training College, Nalerigu	✓			✓		✓								✓	
9.	Nurses Training College, Damongo	✓					✓								✓	
10.	Technical University College, Tamale (BSC & DIP)	✓ *														✓
	TOTAL	7	2	1	5	2	4	-	-	-	-	-	-	-	3	9	1

BASIC PROGRAMMES

RGN - Registered General Nursing

RMN - Registered Mental Nursing

RCN - Registered Community Nursing

RM - Registered Midwifery

OTHER KEYS

* - Bachelor of Science (BSc)

- Training Curtailed

AUXILIARY PROGRAMMES

NAP - Nurse Assistant (Preventive)

NAC - Nurse Assistant (Clinical)

POST AUXILIAY MIDWIFERY

MID -Post NAC/NAP Midwifery

EN - Emergency Nursing

POST BASIC NURSING (PROGRAMMES)

OPN - Ophthalmic Nursing

CCN - Critical care Nursing

PON - Peri-Operative Nursing

PHN - Public health Nursing

ENT - Ear Nose & Throat Nursing

PN - Paediatric Nursing

LIST OF APPROVED NURSING AND MIDWIFERY TRAINING INSTITUTIONS AND PROGRAMMES
UPPER EAST REGION

NO.	NAME OF SCHOOL	PROGRAMME													OWNERSHIP	
		BASIC				AUXILIARIES		POST BASIC NURSING						POST NAC/NAP MIDWIFERY	STATE	PRIVATE
		RGN	RCN	RMN	RM	NAP	NAC	CCN	PON	ENT	PHN	OPN	PN	MID		
1.	Nurses Training College Bolgatanga	✓													✓	
2.	Presbyterian Nurses Training College,Bawku	✓													✓	
3.	Nursing and Midwifery Training College, Zuarungu	✓					✓								✓	
4.	Midwifery Training School, Bolgatanga				✓									✓	✓	
5.	Community Health Nurses Training College, Navrongo		✓			✓									✓	
	TOTAL	3	1	-	1	1	1	-	-	-	-	-	-	1	5	0

BASIC PROGRAMMES

RGN - Registered General Nursing

RMN - Registered Mental Nursing

RCN - Registered Community Nursing

RM   - Registered Midwifery

OTHER KEYS

*   - Bachelor of Science (BSc)

- Training Curtailed

AUXILIARY PROGRAMMES

NAP - Nurse Assistant (Preventive)

NAC - Nurse Assistant (Clinical)

POST AUXILIAY MIDWIFERY

MID -Post NAC/NAP Midwifery

EN - Emergency Nursing

POST BASIC NURSING (PROGRAMMES)

OPN - Ophthalmic Nursing

CCN - Critical care Nursing

PON - Peri-Operative Nursing

PHN - Public health Nursing

ENT - Ear Nose & Throat Nursing

PN - Paediatric Nursing

LIST OF APPROVED NURSING AND MIDWIFERY TRAINING INSTITUTIONS AND PROGRAMMES
UPPER WEST REGION

NO.	NAME OF SCHOOL	PROGRAMME													OWNERSHIP	
		BASIC				AUXILIARIES		POST BASIC NURSING						POST NAC/NAP MIDWFERY	STATE	PRIVATE
		RGN	RCN	RMN	RM	NAP	NAC	CCN	PON	ENT	PHN	OPN	PN	MID		
1.	Nurses Training College, Jirapa	✓													✓	
2.	Midwifery Training School, Jirapa.				✓									✓	✓	
3.	Midwifery Training School, Tumu				✓									✓	✓	
4.	Midwifery Training School, Nandom				✓									✓	✓	
5.	Community Health Nurses Training School, Jirapa		✓			✓									✓	
6.	Nurses Training College, Wa	✓					✓								✓	
7.	Nurses Training College, Lawra	✓					✓								✓	
	TOTAL	3	1	-	3	1	2	-	-	-	-	-	-	3	7	0

BASIC PROGRAMMES

RGN - Registered General Nursing

RMN - Registered Mental Nursing

RCN - Registered Community Nursing

RM   - Registered Midwifery

OTHER KEYS

*   - Bachelor of Science (BSc)

- Training Curtailed

AUXILIARY PROGRAMMES

NAP - Nurse Assistant (Preventive)

NAC - Nurse Assistant (Clinical)

POST AUXILIAY MIDWIFERY

MID -Post NAC/NAP Midwifery

EN - Emergency Nursing

POST BASIC NURSING (PROGRAMMES)

OPN - Ophthalmic Nursing

CCN - Critical care Nursing

PON - Peri-Operative Nursing

PHN - Public health Nursing

ENT - Ear Nose & Throat Nursing

PN - Paediatric Nursing

REFERENCES

1. The Power of Purpose (The Story of Terry Fox) By David McNally.

2. Eden Prairie, Minnesota: Wilson Learning Corp. 612-944-2880

3. Even Eagles Need A Push by David McNally. Eden Prairie, Minnesota: Transform Press, 1990.

4. In Search of the Invincible Forces by George Addair. Phoenix, Arizona: Vector Publications, 1985.

5. The Power of Focus by Jack Canfield, Mark Victor Hansen and Les Hewitt. Benin City Nigeria: Joint Heirs Publications.

6. www.moe.gov.gh

7. www. nmcgh.org

8. www.ntc.gov.gh

9. Don't Sweat the Small Stuff...and it's all stuff by Richard Carlson. Bolton, Ontario: H. B. Fenn & Co., 1997.

10. Don't Worry, Make Money by Richard Carlson. New York, New York: Hyperion, 1997.

11. Future Diary br Mark Victor Hansen. Costa Mesa, California: Mark Victor Hansen and Associates, 1985.

12. How to Handle a Major Crisis by Peter J. Daniels, Ann Arbor, Michigan: Tabor House Publishing, 1987.

13. How to Reach Your Life Goals by Peter J. Daniels, Ann Arbor, Michigan: Tabor House Publishing, 1987.

14. The Seasons of Life by Jim Rohn. Austin, Texas: Discovery Publications, 1981.

15. Work for a Living and Still be Free to Live by Eileen McDargh, New York, New York: Time books, Division of Random House, 1985.

16. Google Images.

www.ingramcontent.com/pod-product-compliance
Lightning Source LLC
Chambersburg PA
CBHW052108150726
48002CB00006B/2272